FOREST CLUB

A YEAR OF ACTIVITIES, CRAFTS, AND EXPLORING NATURE

KRIS HIRSCHMANN
ILLUSTRATED BY MARTA ANTELO

words & pictures

Quarto is the authority on a wide range of topics.

Quarto educates, entertains and enriches the lives of our readers—enthusiasts and lovers of hands-on living.

www.quartoknows.com

First published in 2019 by
words & pictures,
an imprint of The Quarto Group.
6 Orchard Road, Suite 100
Lake Forest, CA 92630
T: +1 949 380 7510
F: +1 949 380 7575
www.QuartoKnows.com

Consultant: Anna Sharratt
Designer: Clare Barber
Editor: Emily Pither
Editorial Director: Laura Knowles
Art Director: Susi Martin
Creative Director: Malena Stojic
Publisher: Maxime Boucknooghe

A CIP record for this book is available from the Library of Congress.

ISBN: 978-1-78603-881-4

Manufactured in Guangdong, China CC042019
9 8 7 6 5 4 3 2 1

MIX
Paper from responsible sources
FSC® C008047
FSC www.fsc.org

PICTURE CREDITS
Alamy: 60r Valentyna Chukhlyebova, 74l Timo Viitanen, 74tr Alfio Scisetti, 74br Zoonar GmbH, 75bl Elena Elisseeva, 75tr Andrew Roland, 75br Redmond Durrell.
Getty: 38tl Foodcollection, 58tr zennie, 59l Elenarts, 61br MediaProduction.
Shutterstock: 8l MiniStocker, 8tr Vaclav Volrab, 8br Guliveris, 9l Zerbor, 9b Zerbor, 9tr StudioByTheSea, 10tl Igor Sokolov (breeze), 10cl Quang Ho, 10bl Albo003, 10c yevtushenko serhii, 10br SasaStock, 11tl alias612, 11l Steven R Smith, 11bl Labrador Photo Video, 11tc Fotofermer, 11b By jopelka, 11tr vvoe, 11cr Fedorov Oleksiy, 11r Iuri, 34tl kelifamily, 34l AS Food studio, 34r Madlen, 34br TunedIn by Westend61, 38 grafvision, 38b osoznanie.jizni, 38r Dionisvera, 38cr YK, 40tl Nikolay Petkov, 40tc Madlen, 40tr rsooll, 40-41 ABTOP, Halina Valiushka, Lukasz Szwaj, maravan, 41 LilKar, 41r Platslee, 46tl vilax, 46l Richard Griffin, 46cl La corneja artesana, 46bl vilax, 46cb, 46tr AS Food studio, 46cr junyanjiang, 46br Richard Griffin, 58l Pablo Scapinachis, 58br chuyuss, 59t Zerbor, 60bl Smit, 61t Elenarts, 70tl Manfred Ruckszio, 72tl haraldmuc, 72l railway fx, 72bl Maslov Dmitry, 72c Henrik Larsson, 72br Anest, 73tl Madlen, 73cl Kazakov Maksim, 73bl Kapustin Igor, 73c haraldmuc, 73tr Tikhomirov Sergey, 73cr aarud, 73br Elenamiv.

Contents

Foreword

If you have watched a child throw twigs into a stream or observe a parade of ants, you know that young people are wired to learn through play and exploration outdoors. But children's connection to nature is at an all-time low, crowded out by academic standards, extracurricular activities, and screens. And even if they wanted to get out, many families and communities lack access to safe parks.

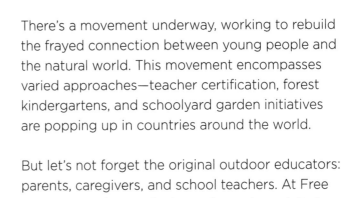

There's a movement underway, working to rebuild the frayed connection between young people and the natural world. This movement encompasses varied approaches—teacher certification, forest kindergartens, and schoolyard garden initiatives are popping up in countries around the world.

But let's not forget the original outdoor educators: parents, caregivers, and school teachers. At Free Forest School, we talk about the caring adults in kids' lives as potential "protectors of nature play." We believe **discovering the natural world should be a part of every childhood**. By shifting adult attitudes and building awareness around the need for nature play in the healthy development of a child, we work to increase children's access to the natural world— and their time to relax and enjoy it.

This beautiful book reminds us that nature is everywhere: Plants can be grown on a doorstep; birds, insects, and small animals thrive in even the

most urban settings. Weather comes and goes; the seasons cycle on. By shifting our thinking, we can nurture a nature connection in a variety of settings and without the help of a formal program. When families come together through a forest club or school, they create a sense of community and routine connected with nature play.

Why does nature matter so much for kids? Study after study has shown that time in nature can have a positive impact on physical health, mental health, and development. **Kids who play in nature are happy, curious, focused, and ready for school.** And an early love of the natural world nurtures the next generation of environmental stewards and leaders.

You need not be an expert to encourage a love of nature in children. In fact, it's best to adopt a learner's mind-set, one of questioning and curiosity, and make time and space for a child's natural sense of wonder to develop. **Carving out unstructured time to observe nature is one of the greatest gifts we can give the children in our lives.** May this book inspire many happy hours of doing "not much"—and everything—in nature together!

Anna Sharratt
Founder of Free Forest School

Summer

Trees in Summer

When you enter the summer forest, tall trees are the first things you will notice. They gently block the sunlight, welcoming you into the forest's cool, dim depths. What types of trees might you see on a walk in the woods?

Birch

Birch trees are delicate and irregular in shape. They are easy to recognize by their paperlike bark, which peels off in sheets. Let nature do this job—never peel off birch paper yourself. It's bad for the tree.

BIRCH

OAK

Oak

Oak trees are usually tall, with spreading canopies of leaves. The bark is gray, rough, and wrinkled. There are about 600 oak species. Oak trees produce acorns that pitter-patter to the ground in the fall. Watch your head!

Ash

Ash trees are medium sized and fluffy. You can identify them by their branches and leaves. Ash branches are smooth and gray. Small shoots emerge from a main branch in opposite pairs. Ash leaves are made up of small, green leaflets on a long stem. The oval-shaped leaflets are arranged in pairs, with an odd one at the end.

ASH

Beech

Look up . . . and up, and up. A beech tree is towering above you! Beech trees can grow up to 160 feet tall. They have smooth, silver-gray bark and dangling, fluffy, fingerlike growths called catkins. Beech trees like dry soil and shade, so you're unlikely to find any near ponds, rivers, or clearings. Delve deep into the forest to find a beech.

BEECH

WILLOW

Willow

Duck through the hanging branches of a willow tree and discover the quiet green space inside. Willows like damp soil and often grow near ponds or streams.

HORSE CHESTNUT

Horse Chestnut

Horse chestnut trees are tall and sturdy. On big, old trees, the branches are curled up at the tips. Horse chestnuts grow spiky green balls that fall to the ground. Crack open the ball to find a hidden treasure inside—a shiny brown conker.

ROWAN

Leaf Types

As you stroll by the trees, look around. Watch the leaves rustling and swaying in the breeze. To get a better look, pick up freshly fallen leaves. If a tree has low-hanging branches, you can examine its leaves right on the tree. Can you find any of the common leaves on this page? Shape, size, and color are all clues to a leaf's identity.

MAGNOLIA

CHESTNUT

HOLLY

LILAC

LINDEN

POPLAR

BIRCH

WILLOW

ELM

OAK

MAPLE

ASH

ASPEN

LEAVE THE LEAVES

Trees need their leaves to stay healthy, so don't pluck living leaves from their branches. Leaves absorb sunlight and turn it into food for the tree. Leaves also absorb some gases from the air and release others when the tree is done with them. It's like breathing. Listen closely. Can you hear the trees breathing around you?

11

What's in a Leaf?

Although leaves come in many shapes and sizes, they all have the same basic parts. Collect several leaves of different types. Look closely. Use a magnifying glass, if you like. Can you identify the parts shown in the picture?

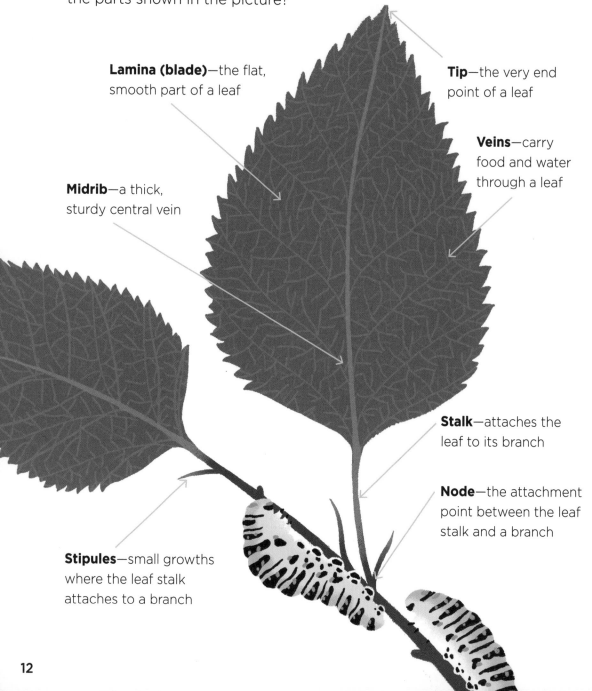

Lamina (blade)—the flat, smooth part of a leaf

Tip—the very end point of a leaf

Veins—carry food and water through a leaf

Midrib—a thick, sturdy central vein

Stalk—attaches the leaf to its branch

Node—the attachment point between the leaf stalk and a branch

Stipules—small growths where the leaf stalk attaches to a branch

ACTIVITY:
Leaf Rubbing

Fallen leaves wither, dry out, and break apart. But you can capture the beauty of leaves by making colorful rubbings on pieces of paper. It's a keepsake that you can bring home and treasure forever.

How to do it

1 Set a leaf on a hard, flat surface. A clipboard would work well. Smooth it out as much as possible.

2 Lay a piece of thin white paper on top of the leaf.

3 Gently rub the long side of a crayon or pastel on the paper over the leaf. The leaf shape will start to appear.

4 Gently rub all areas of the leaf until the image is complete. Experiment with your rubbing pressure. Harder pressure will produce a darker, sharper image. However, too much pressure will make details hard to see.

5 Repeat as many times as you like with different leaves and colors on different parts of the paper.

On a Pond

As you walk through the forest, you may spy a pond sparkling and glinting in the afternoon sunlight. Approach quietly. You wouldn't want to scare away any wonderful creatures that might have come to the pond to drink, swim, or just enjoy the day. What do you think you might see?

Wading Birds

In the shallow water near the pond's edge, wading birds step slowly. They poke their long beaks into the water to grab tasty plants, fish, and insects. Can you spot a bird grabbing a midday snack?

Frogs

CROOOOAAAAK! It's a frog, staring at you with its big, round eyes. Look along the water's edges in grassy or leafy areas for this pond dweller. Can you see a sudden splash? That may have been a startled frog leaping into the water.

Water Striders

Water striders are insects that walk on water. They are so small and light that they do not break the water's surface. Can you see little bugs scooting around on the water? Look out for the tiny ripples they make in the water as they travel.

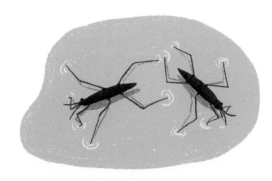

Swimming Birds

Ducks paddle across the surface of ponds, quacking and diving. Angry geese and graceful swans are swimmers, too. Count the swimming birds you see. One, two, three . . . how many will you spy?

Pond Plants

Animals aren't the only life on a pond. You can find many water-loving plants here, too. Colorful lilies, with their spreading pads, float on the pond's surface. Cattails and grasses nod on the banks. Duckweed forms a green mat that ducks may swim through, leaving twisting trails of clear water behind them. How many types of plants can you spot around a pond?

Below the Surface

If you could plunge below a pond's surface, you would find even more living creatures lurking in the cool, green depths. What might you see on your watery journey?

Fish

Slippery, scaly fish wriggle their way through the pond's waters. Pike, trout, carp, and many other types of fish are pond dwellers. They can be big or small, depending on their age and species. Peer into the depths. Can you see a big fish? How about a small fish?

Leeches

Leeches have a bad reputation, and really, that's no surprise. They bite other pond creatures and suck their blood. If you wade in the shallows, watch out—you could become a leech's victim. Can you spy any dark, wormlike creatures in the water near a pond's edge?

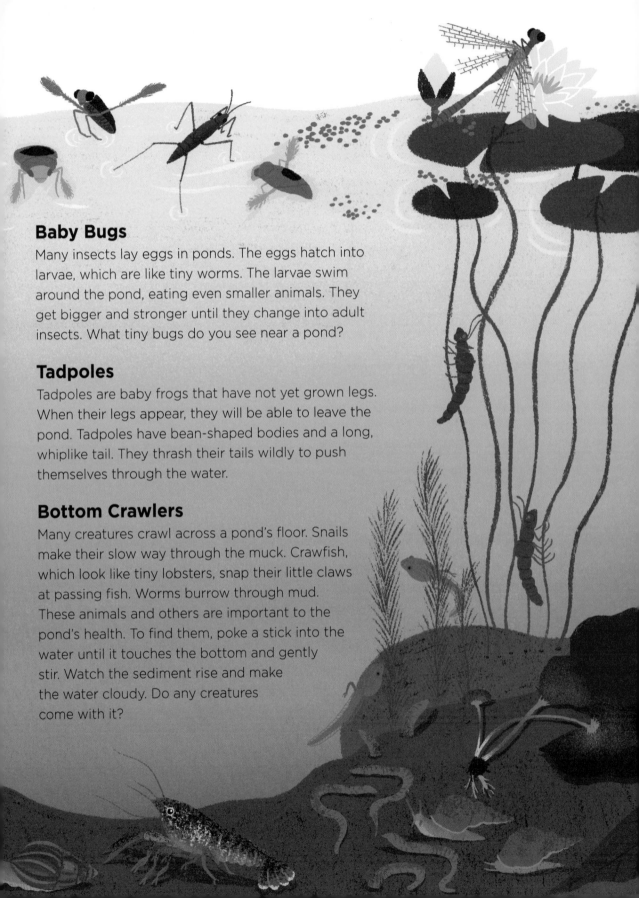

Baby Bugs

Many insects lay eggs in ponds. The eggs hatch into larvae, which are like tiny worms. The larvae swim around the pond, eating even smaller animals. They get bigger and stronger until they change into adult insects. What tiny bugs do you see near a pond?

Tadpoles

Tadpoles are baby frogs that have not yet grown legs. When their legs appear, they will be able to leave the pond. Tadpoles have bean-shaped bodies and a long, whiplike tail. They thrash their tails wildly to push themselves through the water.

Bottom Crawlers

Many creatures crawl across a pond's floor. Snails make their slow way through the muck. Crawfish, which look like tiny lobsters, snap their little claws at passing fish. Worms burrow through mud. These animals and others are important to the pond's health. To find them, poke a stick into the water until it touches the bottom and gently stir. Watch the sediment rise and make the water cloudy. Do any creatures come with it?

ACTIVITY:
Peek into a Pond

From above, it is hard to see far into a pond. This simple viewer will give you a fish's-eye view of the underwater world. You'll need to step into shallow water to get a really good view, so it's best to wear waterproof boots for this activity.

YOU WILL NEED

- Clean, empty 2-liter plastic drink bottle
- Clear plastic wrap
- Elastic band
- Scissors

How to do it

1 Remove the wrapper from the drink bottle. Carefully cut off the top and bottom of the bottle so you have a clear tube. Ask an adult to help with the cutting.

2 Cover one open end with plastic wrap.

3 Use a tight elastic band to secure the wrap.

4 Push the plastic wrap end of the bottle into the water. Look down through the top of the bottle. The wrap will bow upward, creating a lens that magnifies everything below. What do you see?

ACTIVITY:
Pond in a Cup

This technique will let you take an even closer look at some aquatic minibeasts. When you're done looking, return the water—and any tiny critters it contains—to the pond.

YOU WILL NEED

- Inexpensive aquarium net
- Clear plastic cup
- Scissors
- Magnifying glass
- Flashlight

How to do it

1 Use scissors to snip a hole in the bottom of the net. You want a hole about the same size as the bottom of the plastic cup. Don't make it too big!

2 Poke the cup down through the hole until most of the cup has gone through. As the cup gets wider, it should get harder to push, and soon it will be stuck tight.

3 Dip the net and cup into a pond. Swish it back and forth, back and forth.

4 Using the net, pull the cup out of the water. Hold it upright so the water doesn't spill. You do not have to take the cup out of the net; just let the net hang to one side, out of the way.

5 Hold the cup in direct sunlight or shine a flashlight through the water to light things up. Look with your bare eyes, then look again with a magnifying glass. Can you see little beasties moving in the water? What do you observe?

19

Minibeasts

In the forest, minibeasts fly, crawl, and creep. They may be small, but it's not much of a challenge to find them—they're everywhere! How many of these common minibeasts can you spot?

FLYING MINIBEASTS
Butterflies

Butterflies flitter about on colorful wings. These minibeasts have delicate bodies, rest with upright wings, and are active during the daytime.

Bees and Wasps

Bees buzzzzzz from flower to flower, collecting pollen for food. Wasps are hunters that prey on smaller minibeasts. Both bees and wasps can sting, so keep your distance!

Mosquitoes

What's that high-pitched whine? It's a mosquito circling your head, looking for some bare skin to bite. Mosquitoes have long mouthparts that they poke into other animals' flesh. They suck up blood, like they're drinking a milkshake through a straw. Yum!

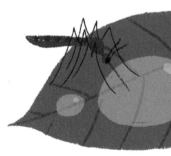

Dragonflies

Dragonflies have long bodies and see-through wings. They come in many different jewel-like colors. They have two enormous, many-lensed eyes. They often hover over bodies of water, looking for snacks swimming below. They may land right on your arm, if you hold still. They are harmless, so relax and enjoy the company.

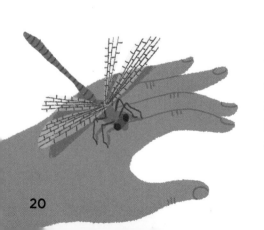

CRAWLING MINIBEASTS
Spiders

Spiders are not insects. They are arachnids, and they have eight legs instead of six. Many spiders spin webs. If you go outdoors in the early morning while it's still dewy, you might see their webs hanging with delicate dew drops. Some spiderwebs are carefully built orbs; others are tangled messes. Look for spiders and their silk-spun homes.

Beetles

Beetles can fly—they have wings hidden beneath their hard shells. But mostly they crawl around on the ground. There are 400,000 types of beetles. Which types live in your local area?

Centipedes

Centipedes have lots and lots of little legs that help them to get around. They like to live in damp soil and leaf litter, under stones and dead wood, and inside logs. Some centipedes have pinching claws and can nip you, so don't touch.

Ants

Ants are busy, busy, busy! They skitter across the ground searching for food. They carry the food back to their nest in long lines. Peek under rocks or rotting wood to find ants hard at work.

LEAPING AND CREEPING MINIBEASTS
Grasshoppers

As minibeasts go, grasshoppers are big! They have strong bodies with long, powerful hind legs. If you startle a grasshopper, it will hop away with a mighty leap.

Caterpillars

Caterpillars look a bit like worms, but they aren't. They are baby butterflies and moths. Caterpillars eat and grow and eat and grow and eat and grow. When they get big enough, they will rest and change into their adult form.

Snails and Slugs

Snails and slugs are similar, but snails have shells and slugs do not. Both minibeasts glide and wriggle slowly from place to place on a trail of slime. They need the slime to protect their soft, squishy bodies from damage.

Worms

Worms prefer to stay underground. But sometimes, especially after a rain, you may find them in open air. Worms are burrowers that chew and churn soil. They are vital to soil health.

ACTIVITY:
Watching Minibeasts

You can watch any larger minibeast as it goes about its regular activities. To see the really itsy-bitsy ones, though, you'll need to get a bit more creative. Here's one easy and safe way to put minibeasts on display.

How to do it

1 Spread your white cloth on the ground beneath a bunch of flowers, tall grasses, or shrubbery.

2 Wearing your gardening gloves and a long-sleeved shirt to protect your arms, gently but firmly shake the plants. You can run your fingers up and down through the plants as well, if you like, taking care not to damage them.

3 Look at the cloth to see if any minibeasts have fallen down. If they have, observe them with the magnifying glass. The white background will make them easy to see.

4 Move the cloth to another area and repeat as many times as you like.

Out and About

Let's move from minibeasts to maxi beasts! What bigger animals might you see on a morning or afternoon walk? Lots of creatures are just waiting to welcome you into their home. If you want to see them, be very quiet . . . you might even sit still in one spot. Be patient. It will take time, but soon the animals will feel safe enough to emerge.

Birds

In the daytime, the forest is alive with birds. Songbirds flit from tree branch to tree branch, cocking their little heads and warbling sweet tunes. Woodpeckers jackhammer tree trunks with their sturdy beaks. At the forest's edge, hunting birds like hawks and kestrels soar and swoop.

Foxes

Foxes have sharp noses, pointy ears, and bushy tails. They are most active at dawn and dusk, but you may see them in full daylight, too. Keep your eyes open for these furry creatures.

Rabbits

Fluffy rabbits leave their dens in the early morning and evening, when the light is dim and the world is quiet. They nibble vegetation calmly. If danger approaches, lickety-split— back into their dens they hop.

Deer

Graceful deer graze in the dappled sunlight near forests' edges. Deer are gentle and wary and tend to stick together. If you see one deer, there's a good chance more are nearby. Look around—they are well camouflaged and can be hard to spot.

Snakes

In nearly any forest, there are bound to be snakes. Most are harmless, but some have a venomous bite. If you see a snake, watch it and enjoy it— from a distance.

Squirrels

Squirrels chitter-chatter in the trees and twitch their furry tails when people approach. See those beady eyes peeking sideways at you? The squirrel will pretend to ignore you, but he knows you're there. Get too close, and zoom! Up the tree he will scamper.

The Forest at Night

When night falls, many animals go to sleep, but others are just waking up and a whole new crew takes over. With a grown-up, take a night walk through the woods. What might you see and hear on your dark journey?

Owls

Hoot, hoot! Owls are on the prowl. Owls are nighttime birds that fly silently on thickly feathered wings. Shine a flashlight up into the tree canopy. Can you spot shining eyes peering down at you?

Wood Mice

Wood mice are small and quiet. They stick to heavy cover, where they will be safer from nighttime predators. These habits make them very difficult to spot. Find a still place and sit silently. Watch and wait—maybe you'll get lucky.

Foxes

Some foxes emerge from their dens at dusk and roam all night long, searching for food. Many foxes prowl in urban areas as well—when night-time comes, you might be able to see a fox slinking down the street.

Bats

Bats are small, winged mammals that take to the air at night. You'll find them at the edges of the forest, where there is plenty of space to swoop and circle. If you are very still and very quiet, you may hear them squeaking. They use their squeaks like radar to help them find food.

Moths

Moths flitter and flutter through the forest trees. Unlike butterflies, moths are active at night. Moths have plump bodies—sometimes bats like to eat them as a snack!

Wild Boar

Wild boar are native to Europe, Asia, and parts of the United States and Australia. They are not quiet. They tromp through bushes with a loud crashing, bashing, and cracking. These big, wild pigs can be grouchy, so keep your distance if you hear a boar—or any large animal—approaching in the night.

Shelters

Whether you are camping out in a forest or playing in a park after school, shelters are fun to make. They keep you warm and also protect you from the elements. There are lots of ways to make a quick shelter. It mostly depends on the materials you are carrying and what natural items you can find around you.

Fallen Tree Shelter

Sometimes tree trunks crack and the upper part of the tree tumbles down. The branches and leaves form a natural canopy that you can crawl beneath. Push the inner branches to the sides to make room for yourself, then find extra branches and lean them against the tree to thicken the canopy.

Lean-to

To make a lean-to shelter, lean thick, leafy branches against a big boulder or another solid object. Add smaller branches to thicken the wall. Crawl into the gap beneath the branches to stay safe and warm.

A-frame

An A-frame shelter is like a lean-to without the side wall. Start by finding two sturdy branches about 5 feet (1.5 meters) long, and one about 8 feet (2.5 meters) long. Use twine to lash the branches together, then lean smaller branches against both sides of the frame to create leafy walls.

ACTIVITY:
Build a Tarp Shelter

A tarp shelter is easy and fun to build. Best of all, it's waterproof. You can make one in minutes with just a few basic supplies.

YOU WILL NEED

- A waterproof tarp
- 13–16 feet (4 to 5 meters) of rope
- Heavy rocks (find these outside)

How to do it

1 Find two trees about 10 feet (3 meters) apart. Tie your rope around both trees, pulling it as tight as possible.

2 Drape your tarp over the rope. Adjust it so it hangs down evenly on both sides.

3 Use heavy rocks to weigh down both sides of your tarp. Pull the sides outward as you do this so the tarp forms an upside-down V shape.

4 You're done! Crawl into your handy-dandy shelter and enjoy being out of the elements.

Fall

Fruits of Fall

The forest bursts with bounty when autumn arrives. Plants hang heavy with fruits that started growing months earlier. Now they are finally full and ripe. What harvest-ready goodies might you find on a walk through the woods?

CAUTION! Some wild fruits are good to eat, but many are not. Some are even poisonous. **NEVER** eat anything you find without adult help and permission.

BERRIES
Blackberries and raspberries

Both of these berries have many juice-filled lobes. They grow on bushes and are good to eat, after washing.

Blackthorn berries

Blackthorn berries are deep blue and cloudy in color. Although they are edible, they can be bitingly bitter. Freeze and then thaw the berries to bring out their sweetness.

Rose hips

Rose hips are the fruits of the rose plant. They are delicious when made into jams and jellies. They can also be eaten raw, but watch out for the hairs inside. They'll tickle your tongue.

TREE FRUITS
Crabapples

Crabapple trees are usually small, with twisted trunks and gnarled limbs. They can be found throughout the world's forests. In the fall, they can be heavy with red, yellow, and orange fruit.

Plums

Wild plums are much smaller than the ones you buy in stores. They look a bit like grapes and are smooth, hairless, and round-oblong shaped. Not all plums are purple—they can also be red, yellow, or even green. If you pluck one from a tree and open it up, you'll find a rough, flat stone inside.

YEW

Danger! Poison!

Along with edible fruit, the fall forest is full of poisonous berries. Many of these berries are colorful and pretty to look at. Enjoy the spectacular colors and shapes of these fruits—but don't touch.

Yew

Bright orange yew berries have a large opening in one end. But watch out—the seed inside is deadly poisonous.

Holly

Holly berries add a splash of color wherever they grow. These solid little beauties are a treat for the eyes, but not the tongue.

POKEBERRY

HOLLY

Pokeberries

Pokeberries are easy to recognize by their vivid purple stems. These dark, shiny berries grow on low, spreading bushes with large green leaves.

NIGHTSHADE

Nightshade

Nightshade berries are glossy deep purple to black in color. They hang in clusters from tiny stems, looking like bunches of miniature eggplants.

ACTIVITY:
Berry Painting

Long before people could buy art supplies in stores, they used berry juice as paint. Try it yourself with materials you find in the forest.

This isn't just fun, it's a useful skill. You never know when you might need to write a message in the woods—or just when the creative urge might strike.

YOU WILL NEED

- Berries (blueberries, blackberries, cherries, or raspberries, are good choices)
- Clear jar and spoon for each type of berry
- Water
- Plastic gloves
- Paintbrush
- White paper

How to do it

1 Put on plastic gloves to protect your hands. Carefully collect a small handful of berries, with adult supervision and help.

2 Put the berries into a jar. Add water until the berries are just covered.

3 Use a spoon to smash and stir the berries until the juice has mixed with the water.

4 Let the berries sit for a while, stirring occasionally. The longer you let them sit, the stronger the color will become.

5 Dip a paintbrush into the jar and use your berry paint to create a masterpiece on a piece of white paper.

Seeds

In the fall, many plants start to release seeds as they prepare for winter. Each seed contains everything it needs to grow into a new plant when the time and conditions are right. Seeds come in many shapes and sizes, and they spread in different ways. They find new places to rest for the winter and, hopefully, to survive until spring.

On the Air

Some seeds spread through the air. They drift on the wind, blowing here and there until they finally come to rest.

SEED HUNT

Look for seeds in the forest. How many different types can you find?

Floating Away

Some seeds drop into running water. They drift away on streams, rivers, lakes, and ocean currents. The water carries them to new places, where they may take root and grow. In this way, forests grow and expand.

Hitching a Ride

Some seeds are covered in tiny hooks. They attach themselves to animals' fur—or your clothes. They hitch a ride to a new place.

Nuts

Nuts are a type of seed. They tumble from trees and bushes in the fall. Like all seeds, a nut contains the information and materials it needs to grow into a new plant. If a nut ends up in a good growing area, it will rest all winter long—then sprout in the spring, when warmer weather arrives.

WALNUT

Walnuts are delicious. The soft, fleshy nut is protected by a tough case that is hard to crack open.

ACORN

Acorns fall from oak trees. They are too bitter for most people, but many animals love them. The top of an acorn, called the cupule, looks a bit like a hat or a cap.

CHESTNUT

BEECHNUT

Sweet chestnuts hide inside soft-spiked cases. People all over the world eat them as a tasty treat. Forest critters like them, too.

Beechnuts come from beech trees. Like sweet chestnuts, these nuts are protected by spiky cases.

HAZELNUT

Hazelnuts are round. They are protected by smooth, reddish-brown shells. The shells crack open by themselves when the nuts are ripe.

ANIMAL AID

Animals such as squirrels and birds help to spread nuts. They pluck nuts from plants or pick them up after they have fallen. They bury or hide the nuts to prepare for the long, hard winter ahead. They intend to come back and eat them later—but sometimes they forget. The buried nuts sit so long that they finally sprout into new plants.

ACTIVITY:
Nut Collecting

Although animals love nuts, they can't collect them all—trees make way too many! Next time you're out and about during fall, challenge a friend to a nut-collecting competition and see who can find the most. Can you spot any of the nuts shown on page 38? See how many different types of nut you can find!

Tips

1 Look on the floor for fresh, fallen nuts.

2 To work out the type of nut, try to identify the tree it came from.

3 Try using a magnifying glass to get a closer look.

ROWAN

RED OAK

BIRCH

Fall Leaves

In autumn, days get shorter and nights get longer. Trees sense the change in sunlight, and they start preparing for winter. A glorious process of color change begins.

Step 1: Turning Off

A tree starts "turning off" its leaves. It grows a special layer of cells to form a barrier between its leaves and branches.

Step 2: Green Gone

Leaves contain a green chemical called chlorophyll. When cold weather arrives, trees stop making new chlorophyll and green leaves start to fade.

ACER

BEECH

Step 3: Other Colors Emerge

The old chlorophyll breaks down and other colors, such as reds, yellows, oranges, and browns, become visible.

Step 4: Colors Brighten

The colors get brighter as the chlorophyll disappears and sunlight makes the colors even stronger.

Step 5: Leaves Fall

When the barrier between the branches and leaves is complete, the leaves can no longer cling to the tree. A light breeze or a shaking branch knocks them loose and they flutter to the ground.

ACTIVITY:
Leaf Wreath

Leaf wreaths bring a touch of fall color to your front door. Follow these easy instructions to build a wreath one leaf at a time as you move through the forest.

How to do it

1 Before you head outside, prepare your wreath base. Use scissors to cut a circle out of the center of the paper plate, leaving a doughnut shape. It should be about a finger length wide.

3 Continue adding leaves throughout your forest visit. Cover the entire doughnut.

4 When you return home, hang your leaf wreath on your front door.

2 Take your paper doughnut and look for pretty fallen leaves. When you find a leaf you like, use a glue stick to attach it to the doughnut. Dry leaves will stick best.

ACTIVITY:
Leaf Art

Make use of the autumn colors and natural materials to create your own piece of simple land art on the forest floor. Your artwork will naturally disappear, so no clearing up is required!

How to do it

1 Find an area on the floor and move any fallen objects aside to create a clear area to work on.

2 Use your imagination to visualize a pattern and place your natural materials on the ground to create your masterpiece. Experiment with materials, colors, and shapes.

3 Take a photograph of your art to capture it forever—the next time you visit, your artwork will have disappeared.

YOU WILL NEED

- A collection of natural objects and fallen leaves in a variety of types and colors
- An open area

Breaking It Down

More and more leaves fall as autumn wears on and a brilliant blanket builds up, covering the forest floor. Underneath, minibeasts are swarming and material is rotting as everything decomposes, or breaks down.

Where to Look

Go Deep: Find an area where leaves are piled deep. Wearing gloves, gently push the layers of leaves aside. Use your senses—smell the rich humus and crinkle the dried leaves. As you dig deeper, you will find that the leaves are broken, smashed, and gooey. Which minibeasts can you see?

A HEALTHY FOREST

Decomposition is important to the forest's health. When leaves, sticks, and other plant matter break down, their nutrients are released. These chemicals enter the soil. They will rest there all winter long. In the spring, trees and other plants will suck up these nutrients through their roots. This natural fertilizer will help plants to make new leaves and branches. When autumn rolls around, the new material will fall and decompose, and the whole cycle will begin again.

Go Below: Thick fallen branches and logs trap moisture beneath them. Wearing gloves, gently lift these objects and peek under them for signs of rotting. How many types of minibeasts can you find?

Go Damp: Look in damp areas, such as pond edges, for signs of rotting. Can you spot any creepy crawlies?

MINIBEASTS

Many minibeasts aid decomposition by helping to break down fallen leaves and other organic material. These minibeasts are called decomposers.

Which minibeasts can you find?

- Spiders
- Beetles
- Millipedes
- Centipedes
- Slugs
- Snails
- Worms
- Woodlice
- Earwigs

BE CONSIDERATE

It is okay to move things to observe decomposition. When you are done looking, however, put everything back the way you found it. This is important to the health of the forest.

Fungi and Lichen

Fungi and lichen are not plants or animals. They are their own type of organism, or living thing. They help to break down debris on the forest floor. Look around to find these common and helpful organisms.

Fungi

"Fungi" is the plural form of the word fungus. Mushrooms are the most common forest fungi. There are about 14,000 known types! Mushrooms are actually the fruit of underground organisms. They make chemicals that break down fallen leaves and other debris.

Mold is another type of fungus. Mold grows in a fuzzy layer on rotting material. It is a sure sign of decay.

Lichen

Lichen is a mixture of fungus and algae. It often grows in crusty mats, but it can also be stringy or slimy. Lichen comes in many different colors.

LOOK AND COUNT

How many types of mushrooms can you find? How many lichens?

ACTIVITY:
Spore Prints

Mushrooms shed thousands of tiny seeds called spores from their undersides. The spores fall in patterns that match the mushroom's shape. Scientists capture these spore prints to identify the mushrooms they find in the wild.

Here's how to make your own spore prints using just a few simple materials.

YOU WILL NEED

- Fresh mushroom, the type with gills
- Sheet of white paper
- Water
- Cup that is larger than the mushroom's cap
- Hairspray

How to do it

1 With a grown-up's help, cut the stem off the mushroom. Be very careful not to damage the fragile gills.

2 Lay a sheet of white paper on a flat surface where it will not be disturbed. Set the mushroom cap, gills down, on the paper.

3 Put a few drops of water on top of the mushroom. This will help it to open up and release its spores.

4 Cover the mushroom cap with a cup. This will stop air from blowing across the mushroom cap.

5 Let the mushroom cap sit undisturbed for 24 hours. Then lift the cup and the cap. Look at the paper. You should see a colorful spore print in the shape of the mushroom's gills.

6 Spray the spore print with hairspray to preserve it. Turn it into a greeting card or anything else you like.

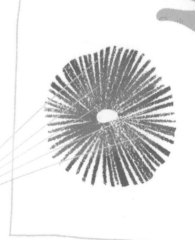

Migration

Many animals cannot survive cold weather. When fall arrives, they head south to spend the winter in a warmer climate. This seasonal movement is called migration. What migrating creatures might you spot in the sky?

Geese

Geese head south in the fall. They travel in small groups, forming a V shape as they fly.

Swallows

Swallows leave their northern homes in August and September. They travel in enormous flocks. Hundreds of thousands of swallows may migrate together.

Swifts

Swifts live on all continents except Antarctica. They migrate twice per year. They head north in the spring, spend the summer in cooler climates, and then return south in the fall. You can see them passing overhead in flocks of up to 10,000 birds.

Arctic Terns

Arctic terns are long-distance champions. They migrate in a zigzag pattern from the Arctic to the Antarctic every year—and back again. That's a round trip of about 44,000 miles (71,000 kilometers)! They rest in coastal areas along the way.

Butterflies and Moths

Some butterflies and moths migrate long distances. Monarch butterflies travel between North and Central America, depending on the time of year. In Britain, the hummingbird hawkmoth flies south when cool weather arrives.

Bats

Some bats migrate in the fall. Most bats fly at night, so it may be hard to spot these critters on the move.

Winter

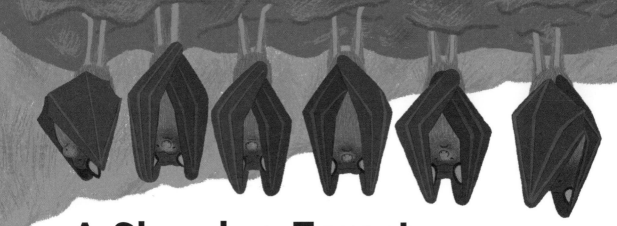

A Sleeping Forest

Instead of migrating, many animals stay put when winter arrives. But the cold weather chills them, and food becomes harder and harder to find. They solve these problems by going into a deep sleep called hibernation. They will hibernate all winter long, waking up just a few times for a quick bite of stored food and a bathroom break. What animals might be quietly hibernating, out of sight, in your forest?

Bats

Bats hibernate in caves, tree hollows, wells, or even people's attics. Their bodies slow down so much that they may only breathe once per hour!

Bears

Bears live mostly in North America, Europe, and Asia. They enter their dens around September and hibernate until spring. They live off stored fat in their bodies during this time.

Ants

Ants hibernate during bitter winter months. They head to warm places, such as under rocks, soil, or even beneath tree bark.

Bumblebees

Bumblebees are warm-weather creatures. They die when the weather turns cold. Only the queen from each colony survives. She hibernates in a hole in the ground. In the spring, she will emerge and start a new colony.

Wood Frogs

When frogs hibernate, their hearts stop beating and ice crystals form in their blood. When spring comes, they wake up, as good as new.

Snakes

Snakes enter a state called brumation, which is like hibernation, but even deeper. They seek cover in places like caves, hollow logs, and under wood piles. Sometimes hundreds of snakes sleep through the winter together. A place where this happens is called a hibernaculum.

Below the Ice

Ponds get very cold in the heart of winter. Sometimes they even freeze over. Below the ice, though, there is still plenty of water—and plenty of life. What would you see if you could peek below the ice?

Moving Slowly

Many fish, such as catfish and carp, are stunned by winter's cold. They enter a state called torpor where their bodies work more slowly. They are alive but very inactive.

Cold but Happy

Other fish, such as trout, like cold water. They stay active all winter long. Below the ice, they hunt and swim.

Digging In

Some creatures burrow into the mud and silt on the pond floor. There they snooze the winter away. Frogs, salamanders, and turtles use this survival strategy to keep them hidden and safe while asleep.

Surface Dwellers

Plants called algae do not mind the cold at all. They grow right on the underside of a pond's icy surface. They thrive on the weak sunlight that filters through the ice.

Buried Roots

The visible parts of pond plants die off when a pond ices over. Below the pond floor, however, the root systems are still alive. They wait for spring warmth to nudge them back into action.

ACTIVITY:
Slowing Down

Unlike some animals, humans do not hibernate, but they do have periods of activity and calm. What happens to your body when you switch from one state to the other? Try this activity to find out for yourself!

YOU WILL NEED
- A quiet, calm place to sit
- Timer, or a clock or watch with a second hand
- Paper and pencil

How to do it

1 Walk around for several minutes to get your body pumped up.

2 Using your timer, count how many breaths you take in one minute. Write down the number.

3 Now take your pulse for one minute or have a grown-up help you. You can feel your pulse in your neck and wrists. Look at the pictures to see how. Write down how many times you feel your heart beat in one minute.

4 Sit or lie in a quiet area where you will not be disturbed. Get completely comfortable. Close your eyes. Breathe deeply and slowly and relax your muscles. Do this for at least five minutes.

5 Repeat steps 2 and 3, moving as little as possible. What changes do you see in your breathing and heart rate? You should find that your body has slowed down quite a bit. You're not hibernating, but it's a start!

Winter Adaptations

Not all animals migrate or hibernate. Some stay awake and active all winter long. Winter animals often change in ways that help them to survive in cold weather. Look carefully at any animals you see roaming out and about. Can you spot any of these winter adaptations?

Camouflage

Colors and patterns that help an animal blend into its surroundings are called camouflage. In snowy areas, some animals turn white in the wintertime. Arctic foxes grow a thick white fur. Snowshoe hares and stoats turn from brown to white when winter arrives. Snowy owls are white year-round, which makes them hard to see in snowy conditions.

Warm Feet

Animals that walk through snow need to keep their feet warm. In winter, many animals with padded feet—like foxes— grow extra fur on their soles. The fur sticks out between their pads. Birds called ptarmigans grow extra feathers on their feet to keep them warm.

Winter Coats

Many animals—like deer and some birds—become extra fluffy when cold weather arrives. Thicker fur and feathers trap body heat. They act like a natural blanket to keep out the chill.

ACTIVITY:
Follow That Critter!

Woodland animals leave marks in fresh snow as they move through the forest. Follow any trails you find and see what you can learn about the animals that made them.

How to do it

1 Head outside the day after a snowfall. Dress warmly before heading out so you don't get cold.

2 Walk quietly so you won't disturb any wildlife. Look around for marks and tracks in the fresh snow.

3 When you find an animal's trail, look closely at the marks. Do you see prints? If so, place a coin on the snow next to a print. Snap a photo. Later, when you look at your pictures, the coin will be a size marker.

4 Follow the trail as far as you can, in either direction. When you reach the end, turn around. Go back the other way as far as you can to make sure you see the trail's entire length.

5 A trail may lead you to an animal's home. If so, keep your distance. Observe through binoculars. If you see movement, quick! Take a picture!

6 Think about the tracks you have found. Use your powers of reasoning. What animal do you think made the tracks? What do you think the animal was doing? Turn to pages 82–83 for a guide to animal tracks.

Evergreen Trees

It is easy to see how evergreen trees got their name—they stay green all winter long. Instead of broad leaves, many of them have needles that never fall off. They bring a welcome splash of color to the stark winter landscape. You'll have to look up high to see if you can find these common, tall evergreens on a chilly midwinter walk through the forest.

Douglas Fir

Douglas firs are tall and stately. Their gray-green needles are short and tightly spaced.

Norway Spruce

The Norway spruce is medium sized and triangular, with a pointed tip. The needles are close together. The needles are softer and more raggedly arranged than those of a Douglas fir.

Scots Pine

The bare trunk of a Scots pine goes up, up, up before finally erupting into a canopy of green needles. The needles are long and soft.

DOUGLAS FIR

SCOTS PINE

NORWAY SPRUCE

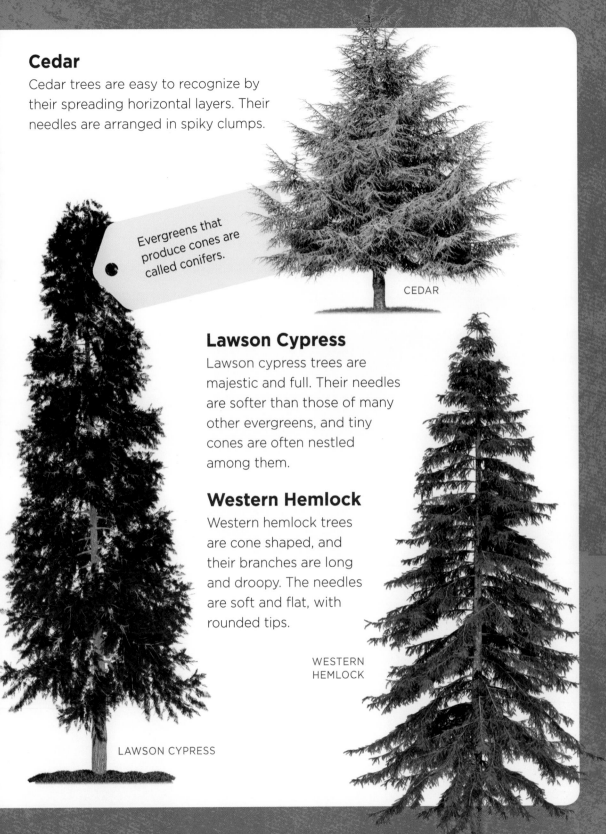

Cedar

Cedar trees are easy to recognize by their spreading horizontal layers. Their needles are arranged in spiky clumps.

Evergreens that produce cones are called conifers.

CEDAR

Lawson Cypress

Lawson cypress trees are majestic and full. Their needles are softer than those of many other evergreens, and tiny cones are often nestled among them.

Western Hemlock

Western hemlock trees are cone shaped, and their branches are long and droopy. The needles are soft and flat, with rounded tips.

WESTERN HEMLOCK

LAWSON CYPRESS

BOX

Down to Earth

You've looked up at the trees. Now look down toward the ground. Many evergreens grow as shrubs or ground cover.

Box

Box, also called boxwood, grows in low, thick shrubs. In formal gardens, it is often trimmed into neat shapes. In the wild, it can relax and grow however it likes. The leaves are small and rounded.

HOLLY

Holly

Young holly plants look like shrubs. Older ones can look more like short, squat trees. Holly's spiky, glossy leaves and bright red berries make this plant a holiday favorite.

JUNIPER

Juniper

Juniper spreads out over the ground in bushy masses. Its grayish needles are sharp, and they stick out from their branches at odd angles. They bear small, round cones that look just like berries.

YEW

LEARN YOUR SHRUBS

Lots of gardeners love to plant evergreen shrubs and low-growing plants. Go to your local garden center. Read the labels and look carefully at the plants. When you get to the forest, you'll know exactly what you are looking at.

Yew

Like holly, yew can look like a shrub or a small tree. It has short, sharp, upturned needles. Sometimes it bears beautiful red berries with poisonous seeds.

Hawthorn

There are different types of hawthorns. The shrub type grows in a scraggly, random mess of branches. It has flat, green leaves.

HAWTHORN

ACTIVITY:
Scents of Nature

Many evergreens contain a sticky substance called resin. Most people think evergreen resins smell wonderful, especially those made by pines, spruces, and firs. Juniper and cypress resin smell great, too. Here's how you can conduct your very own scratch-and-sniff experiment.

YOU WILL NEED

• Conifer needles and leaves

How to do it

1 Pick up a fresh conifer needle or leaf from the ground, if you can find one. If not, carefully pinch off one tiny needle from an evergreen tree or bush. Take as little as possible to avoid damaging the plant.

2 If you are wearing gloves or mittens for warmth, remove them for a moment. Squeeze and pinch the needle between your fingers and crack it with your nails to release the scent.

3 Raise the needle to your nose and take a whiff. You should be rewarded with a strong and delightful scent.

4 Repeat with needles and leaves from other conifers. The scents will be similar, but a little different. Which one is your favorite?

ACTIVITY:
Bark Rubbing

Trees keep their bark all year round, so winter is an ideal time to make picture-perfect rubbings of these lumpy, bumpy coverings. Bark rubbing is a great way to capture the natural world and take a piece of it home with you.

YOU WILL NEED

• Paper
• Crayons or pastels with paper wrappers removed
• Trees

How to do it

1 Hold a piece of paper against a tree trunk.

2 Rub the long side of the crayon or pastel on the paper. The bark's texture will start to appear.

3 Experiment with your rubbing technique. Try rubbing up and down, then side to side. Experiment with the pressure as well. Different methods will yield different results.

4 Keep rubbing until the paper is covered, or until the bark print is as big as you like. You have captured a bit of the winter world.

5 Display your bark rubbings on the wall, use them as wrapping paper, turn them into greeting cards, or do anything else you like with them.

Winter Treasures

In the winter months, the leaves have fallen, the flowers have died, and the woods are barren. Or are they? Not even close. The winter forest is full of treasures just waiting to be found. How many of these winter wonders can you spot?

Icicles

Icicles are spikes of ice that form when dripping water freezes. Icicles start out small and grow over time. If conditions are good, they can become very large. What's the biggest icicle you can find?

Nests

When trees lose their leaves, abandoned nests are easy to spot. Look up. Search for the telltale tangles of twigs and leaves that mark old bird and squirrel nests.

Cones

Evergreens drop spiky cones during the winter. They are often called pine cones, although they do not come only from pine trees. Cones are made of woody scales that arch and spread outward in pretty, regular patterns. The size and the pattern vary from one cone to another. Collect as many types as you can.

Sap

Sap is a sticky substance that flows inside trees, but during freezing weather it stops flowing. If the temperature shifts a bit higher, though—even just a bit above freezing—the sap will start flowing again. It may ooze out of the tree's trunk or branches. Look for flowing sap on warmer winter days.

Galls

Galls are swelling growths on tree branches or trunks. They are caused by damage from insects, bacteria, or fungi. They can be big or small. How many galls can you count?

Hidden Minibeasts

Many minibeasts are active all winter long. Carefully lift logs and rocks to expose the bare soil beneath. Is anything skittering underneath? Make sure to put everything back the way you found it, so your little buddies don't get chilly.

ACTIVITY: Stay Warm!

The longer you spend in the winter woods, the more you'll feel the chill. Even if you're all bundled up, the cold will seep in after a while. Here are some fun activities that will warm you up when you start to shiver.

Play Tag

Tag is a running game, so it will keep you warm and toasty when you're outside exploring nature. Choose one person to be "It." That person tries to touch, or "tag," the other players. The other players try not to be tagged. Anyone who is tagged becomes the new "It." Repeat until all chills are gone.

Make a Trail

Gather an armful of sticks and twigs. Arrange them into arrow shapes on the ground and make a long trail. End the trail with a pinecone or another winter treasure. Can your friends follow the hints you have left and find the prize?

Have a Scavenger Hunt

Make a list of ten things you can find outside—leaves, rocks, moss, twigs, and so on. The winner is the first person to find all ten items.

Do Jumping Jacks

Jumping jacks (or any type of vigorous exercise) will raise your body temperature faster than anything else. Warm up and have fun at the same time.

ACTIVITY:
Steamy Hot Drink

Nothing tastes better than a hot, delicious drink on a freezing cold day. Bring a hot drink with you into the forest for a scrumptious homemade treat.

YOU WILL NEED

- Heatproof flask
- Ingredients
- An adult to help heat the drink

HERE ARE SOME IDEAS:

- Warm milk and a dash of vanilla
- Hot apple juice with a pinch of cinnamon
- Instant hot chocolate, topped with mini marshmallows
- Warm milk, cocoa, and a sprinkle of sugar
- Hot water with a slice of lemon and a drop of honey

Spring

Signs of Spring

Spring begins long before the world bursts into bloom. As winter is drawing to an end, take a walk through the woods. Look carefully—can you spot these signs of the forest coming to life?

Buds

Tree and bush branches form lumpy buds in the fall. The buds rest all winter, but in the early spring, they start to grow, and tiny little leaves or flowers appear. Look for bursting buds when spring arrives.

Seedlings

You might have to push leaf litter aside to find these baby plants emerging from the soil. All plants start as little seedlings—even the tallest trees!

Grass Shoots

Grass shoots are a type of seedling. They are thin, green, and straight. Look for grass shoots growing together on the forest floor.

New Needles

If you can spot a pine tree, look for new needles at the ends of its branches. They are light green and soft.

Color Everywhere

Take a walk up to higher ground and search for the colors of spring. If you gaze out over the forest below, you may see subtle colors emerging, such as yellow, green, pale pink, and purple.

Smell the Sap

Tree sap is a sure sign of spring. It's a sticky substance that flows inside trees when spring approaches and often oozes out through cracks in the tree's bark. It's best to avoid touching sap, but if you want to get closer, why not try smelling it? Some smells sweet and some is sour-smelling depending on the tree. Sap may smell great, but don't put it in your mouth.

Budding Branches

Many trees look stark in early spring, with their leaves stripped away by the chilly winter. But take a closer look at the branches—tiny buds start to emerge in spring, ready to erupt into leaves when the time is right. How many of these common trees can you identify from their twigs? Look for twigs both on the ground and still attached to trees.

BLACKTHORN

OAK

HAWTHORN

LARCH

BEECH

PUSSY WILLOW

LILAC

ASH

ELM

LIME

BIRCH

HORSE
CHESTNUT

Common Flowers

Flowers show that spring has really, truly arrived. Head outside and look out for these common blooms along the forest's edges, where there is plenty of sunlight.

VIOLET

Violet

You're bound to see some little violets out in the forest during spring. They are usually purple or blue and have a sweet scent.

Snowdrop

Snowdrop blossoms dangle from bent stems, like little bells or lamps. They are usually white or greenish-white.

SNOWDROP

Daffodil

Cheerful yellow daffodils are easy to identify! Their bright-colored blooms are a sure sign that spring has sprung. The big central bell makes this flower unique.

DAFFODIL

KEEP IT WILD

Remember that wild flowers shouldn't be picked—they may look lovely, but if everyone picked them and took them home, there wouldn't be any left for others to see.

Primrose

Primroses come in many shapes and colors. The common forest type has heart-shaped petals.

Crocus

Crocus are early bloomers. They sometimes grow through snow! Yellow, lavender, cream, and white are the most common colors.

PRIMROSE

BLUEBELL

CROCUS

Bluebell

Bluebells spend most of the year as bulbs underground and emerge to flower in spring. They have delicate, blue-lilac bell-shaped flowers.

ACTIVITY:
Sprouting Seeds

You can't watch seeds sprout in the forest—it takes too long. But you can plant seeds at home and watch the whole process, from beginning to end!

How to do it

1 Put potting soil or compost into your pot. Dampen the soil with some water.

2 Different seeds need different soil depths and growing conditions. They also take different amounts of time to sprout. Follow the instructions on the seed packet to plant and tend your seeds.

3 If you tend to your seeds well, a seedling will appear! Water and tend the seedling for a week or two. When the little plant has three to four leaves, take it outside and plant it in the ground. With luck, it will grow into a healthy adult plant!

YOU WILL NEED

- Seed packet (from any garden center). Sunflower, cress, and marigold seeds are great choices.
- Potting soil or compost
- Plant pot
- Water

ACTIVITY:
Flower Pressing

Pressed, dried flowers keep their shapes and colors forever. Use this method to capture a little forest magic.

Ask your parents if you can have a flower from your yard, or preserve a flower found on the forest floor.

How to do it

1 Put several flat layers of tissue paper on one sheet of cardboard. Put the flower on the tissue paper.

2 Put several more layers of tissue paper onto the flower. Add the other sheet of cardboard. Press firmly.

3 Put everything between two middle pages of a hardcover book. This will hold everything together.

4 When you get home, set the book on a table in a warm, dry place. Set many heavy books on top of the first book.

5 Let everything sit for two to three weeks. Then carefully open the bottom book and check your flower. It should be flat, dry, and beautiful!

6 Very carefully dab some glue to the back of your flowers and use them to decorate scrapbooks, notebooks, or cards.

Rivers, Streams, and Creeks

In the spring, snow melts and rain falls, so there will be lots of fresh water in the forest. The water swells rivers, streams, and creeks, and the flowing water keeps forests healthy. During your woodland walks, look out for wet pools, puddles, and patches. Listen to the drops of rain pattering on leaves. If you can spot any rivers, streams, or creeks, keep your eye out for running water, plants, and animals.

Running water

Watch running water to see how it flows and where it goes. Water from rain and melting snow has to go somewhere, and rivers, streams, and creeks drain the land. The water runs downhill and collects in bodies of water, such as ponds and lakes.

Plants

Can you see any plants growing near flowing water? Plants need water to survive. Water passes into a tree or plant's roots and is carried up the stem or trunk, all the way up to the leaves.

Animals

Do you see any living creatures in or near flowing water? If you don't see the actual animals, can you spot signs of animal life? Animals get thirsty! Animals such as beavers, voles, and deer come to rivers, streams, and creeks to have a cool drink.

ACTIVITY:
Twig Racing

If you spot a river, stream, or creek during a forest adventure, take a break to play a game of twig racing. You'll need one twig each, and it works best if your twigs are different shapes or sizes so that you can recognize which one belongs to each person.

YOU WILL NEED
• River, stream, or creek
• Small twigs

How to do it

1 Pick a starting point and decide on a finish line that is within sight. Bridges work very well as you can start and finish at either side.

2 Each player should drop a twig into the water at the starting point.

3 Keep an eye on your twig and follow its downstream progress. Some of the twigs may get stuck behind rocks or other obstacles, and some may enter faster parts of the waterway and zoom ahead . . . you just have to go with the flow!

4 The winner is the person whose twig reaches the finish line first.

5 When the race is over, find a new set of twigs and start a new race!

ACTIVITY:
Build a Dam

A dam is any structure, natural or artificial, that blocks the flow of water. To investigate how they work, try making your own simple dam and see how it affects a waterway. This is a great activity to do in a small, narrow stream that you can walk in.

YOU WILL NEED

- Natural building materials, such as rocks and sticks

How to do it

1 Collect loose rocks and sticks and pile them up next to the stream.

2 One by one, place the rocks and sticks in the water. Watch what happens to the water flow with each addition. Does it change course? Back up? Get faster or slower?

3 Experiment with different arrangements and observe what happens as you make changes.

4 When you're ready to stop, remove the rocks and sticks from the water. Return them to the forest and put them back roughly where you found them.

Animal Tracks

Many creatures roam in the forest and leave behind tracks in the mud. What types of animals are wandering in your local area?

Rabbits

Hop, hop, hop! Rabbits plant their big rear feet in front of their smaller front feet with each jump.

Squirrels

Like rabbits, squirrels plant their rear feet first and hop. You can see their little toe prints.

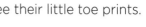

Deer

Deer have hooves. The two dots come from small extra claws at the back of the foot.

Birds

Bird tracks are easy to recognize! Most birds have one clawed toe at the back and three at the front.

Dogs

Not all animals in the forest are wild! Doggie paw prints can be big or small, depending on the pup.

ACTIVITY:
Plaster Casting

Make plaster casts to "save" interesting animal tracks that you find on forest adventures. This activity is an easy and fun way to remember a great day and to show your friends what you spotted.

YOU WILL NEED

- Plaster of Paris (about three heaped tbsp for a small cast)
- Water
- Bendable cardboard strip
- Zip-top plastic bag
- Small shovel
- Small box or other protective container

How to do it

1 Bend a cardboard strip all the way around the print you want to cast. Push it into the mud to hold it in place.

2 Combine one-part water to two-parts plaster of Paris in a zip-top bag.

3 Squeeze the bag to mix the plaster and water.

4 Carefully pour the mixture into the print. The cardboard strip will keep the plaster from running all over the place.

5 Wait about 20 to 30 minutes, until the cast hardens. Use a small shovel to scoop up the cast.

6 Put the cast into a small box to protect it. Later, when you get home, brush as much dirt as you can off the plaster to reveal your preserved animal print.

PLASTER

1kg

ACTIVITY:
Photo Safari

You can also preserve animal tracks without plaster. Photos will help you to remember your discoveries long after you leave the forest. Grab your camera and head out into the wild—you never know what you might find.

How to do it

1 Take close-up photos of any animal tracks you find. You could try including an object to show scale or a ruler to show the size of the track.

2 Check to make sure each image is crisp and clear before moving on. If not, try again to get a better photo.

3 Back home, load the photos onto your computer. They will be bigger and easier to see on your computer screen. Use pages 82–83 or search online to figure out which animals made the tracks.

4 Print your best pictures, if you like. Label them with the time, date, and type of animal. Keep the printouts as a record of your day.

Animal Homes

The forest is full of animals—and just like you, all of these animals need a place to live. Animals, birds, and minibeasts live in all sorts of different places. Look up high and down below. What can you see? Here are some animal homes that you might find.

Bird Nests

In the spring, many birds build nests in trees. The nests are made of twigs, dried grass, moss, and other handy materials. Birds build nests to keep their eggs safe and warm.

BZZZ... BZZZ... BZZZ

Wasp Nests

Some types of wasps build nests from wood pulp. The nests hang from tree branches. When you're out and about, remember to keep your distance from wasp nests. Wasps are dangerous and may sting you if you disturb their nest.

Dreys

Squirrel homes are called dreys, and they are usually built in the forks of tall trees. They are like little round caves, woven from dry leaves and twigs.

Tree Holes

All sorts of animals live in tree holes. Woodpeckers, owls, bats, and squirrels are a few possible residents. Look up high and see who you can spot.

Burrows

Many animals dig burrows in the ground. Rabbits, foxes, chipmunks, and moles all dig burrows. Look down low for entrance holes—big, small, and inbetween, depending on the size of the animal.

New Life

Spring is about new beginnings, change, and growth, and after a long winter, new generations of animals start to appear. Spring is a good time for animals to give birth to young because the weather is often warmer and there is more food available. Look out for these signs of new life.

Fish Fry

Baby fish are called fry. If you come across a pond in the spring, look at the edge of it—if you're lucky enough to be there after a hatch, you may see thousands of little fish fry swimming about in the water.

Frog Spawn

Frog spawn looks like lots of little bubbles sitting on water. Each bubble is an egg and each egg will hatch into a tiny tadpole—a fishlike baby frog.

Baby Birds

Many birds lay eggs in the spring. A mama bird usually sits on the eggs in her nest to keep them warm and safe. When the eggs hatch, the parent birds fly back and forth to find and bring food to the chicks.

Following Mama

Many baby animals follow their mothers until they are old enough to survive on their own. Look for baby ducks, rabbits, deer, and other little critters in the spring. If you spot any, remember to keep your distance so as not to disturb them.

ACTIVITY:
Build a Bird's Nest

To build their nests, birds carefully select natural materials. Then they weave the materials together into the desired shape. Some birds make very intricate structures that can take days to build. Try this activity and build your own bird's nest.

YOU WILL NEED
....
• Natural nest-building materials (such as twigs, grass, leaves, and straw)

How to do it

1 Start by collecting your materials. Think like a bird. Collect anything you think might help you to build a nest.

2 Pile all the materials together on the floor.

3 Using nothing but your fingers, try to shape the materials into a nest. Try making a frame out of twigs, then weaving smaller twigs along with flexible materials, such as straw, through the frame to create a nest shape.

4 Layer the inside of the nest with soft materials.

ACTIVITY:
Three in a Row

The forest supplies everything you need for a fun round of Tic-Tac-Toe. Who will get three in a row and win this two-player game?

YOU WILL NEED

- Four long, straight sticks
- Five game tokens for each player

How to do it

1 Each player finds five natural objects to use as game tokens. Each player should choose a different type of object. For instance, one player might find five rocks, while the other player uses five leaves.

2 Lay the four sticks in a criss-cross pattern on the ground to make the game board.

3 Choose one player to go first. Player One puts a token into any one of the nine spaces made by the sticks.

4 Now it is the second player's turn. Player Two puts a token into any remaining space.

5 Players continue alternating turns. The goal is to get three matching tokens in a row. If a player succeeds, he or she wins the game.

6 To play again, just pick up the tokens and start over. This game is quick, easy, and fun while spending time in the forest.

Sounds of Spring

In the springtime, the forest is busy, busy, busy. If you listen closely, you'll be amazed by all the sounds you can hear! Here are some things you might be able to hear. Can you identify any other sounds?

Birds: Songbirds singing, birds tweeting, crows cawing, geese honking, ducks quacking, owls hooting, woodpeckers pecking, wings beating.

Insects: Mosquitoes whining, cicadas droning, crickets chirping, bees buzzing.

Trees and plants: Pinecones falling, grass swaying, leaves rustling in the breeze.

Water: Rain falling, fish splashing, brooks babbling, waterfalls tumbling, frogs croaking.

Animal movement: Feet scurrying, twigs cracking, leaves crunching, branches shaking, bushes rustling.

Notes for Parents and Teachers

Here are some ideas to help you encourage a love of nature in children.

- ADVENTURE: Going out to explore should be an adventure that is in line with the developmental stage of the child. An adventure for a baby is lying on a blanket underneath trees. For a toddler it is taking a ramble through a park with plenty of time to pick up sticks and investigate. An adventure for a four-year-old might mean climbing the same tree for an hour. Don't wear yourself out planning a grand adventure when something simple will do!

- LET GO: Practice letting go. Given space to do so, kids will take the lead and delight in exploring. Research shows that kids who are free to take risks in their play (such as balancing on stepping stones across a creek) develop responsibility and judgment.

- SLOW DOWN: Abandon the idea of getting to a certain destination. The journey, and the time to explore, are what matter most in cultivating a deep connection to the natural world. When we hustle kids to hike to a given destination in a timely manner, our goals may run counter to young people's natural desire to investigate and sour them on spending time in nature.

- BUILD A ROUTINE: Look for ways to make nature a part of your daily or weekly routine. If nature-based learning is not a part of your school offerings, consider making time before or after school and on weekends. You can do this informally by taking a detour through a park or bird watching on your way to school, or formally by enrolling in an after-school program or starting a family nature club.

- RAIN OR SHINE: An old adage says, "There's no such thing as bad weather, just bad clothing." So, adjust your attitude, layer up, and enjoy exploring no matter the weather.

- MAKE TIME FOR NATURE: It's possible to find aspects of the natural world even in the midst of a packed schedule. Try leaving the house ten minutes early in the morning to look for birds or hunt for icicles. When planning social gatherings, choose an outdoor setting like a park. Park your car or get off transit a few blocks before your destination and enjoy the walk.

- EXPAND YOUR DEFINITION: Embrace the concept of "nearby nature" by noticing living creatures and seasonal changes in your backyard, a nearby park, or on your street.

- FIND COMMUNITY: Research forest schools and outdoor programs in your area—these are great places to meet new people and discover local nature areas.

- KEEP A JOURNAL: Start keeping a nature journal where you record your observations. Kids can carry blank journals and colored pencils, too. A journal should be the child's own book to use in any way they see fit, for things such as making notes, drawing, or adding photos.

- SIT STILL: Try introducing "sit spots" as an activity. Each person finds their own spot to settle down quietly for a set amount of time (five minutes is a good place to start). Prompt observation by asking children to tune into their senses, such as the feeling of breeze on their face or the wind in their hair.

Anna Sharratt
Founder of Free Forest School

Equipment

You don't need expensive equipment to learn about nature—it's about getting outside, exploring, and experimenting. While you might choose to bring some basic tools, leave toys and valuable possessions at home. This inspires creative play with found objects in nature. Here are suggestions for simple tools that might come in handy:

TOOLS

- Pens
- Pencils
- Paper
- Camera
- Magnifying glass
- Binoculars
- Flashlight
- Twine or cord
- Empty plastic containers from the recycling bin, such as 1-quart yogurt tubs
- Scissors
- Pocket knife
- Simple first-aid kit

CLOTHING AND EQUIPMENT

- Backpack
- Water bottle
- Waterproof jacket
- Waterproof footwear
- Long-sleeved top
- Long trousers
- Sweater
- Hat, gloves, and scarf for cold weather
- Hat and sunscreen for warm weather

Further information

For further information about forest schools and options in your local area, these programs are a great place to start:

Free Forest School
www.freeforestschool.org
Letting kids be kids, outdoors. Free Forest School ignites children's innate capacity to learn through unstructured play in nature, fostering healthy development and nurturing the next generation of creative thinkers, collaborative leaders, and environmental stewards.

Forest Schools Kindergarten
www.forestschoolskindergarten.com
Forest Schools Kindergarten gives children the time, space, and freedom to play while immersed in a natural environment.

Forest Schools Education
www.forestschools.com
A Forest School training provider with over 15 years of helping educators change the lives of those around them.

Index